The Seventeenth Chapter

BY JOSLYN CROWL

Copyright 2022 The Seventeenth Chapter by Joslyn D. Crowl

All Rights Reserved. This book is protected by the copyright laws of the United States of America and cannot be copied or reprinted for commercial or personal gain or profit. Editor Heather Wilson.
Photography and design by Joslyn Crowl

TABLE OF CONTENTS

Chapter 1 *Pain Changes People*

Chapter 2 *I Was Just Twelve Years Old*

Chapter 3 *The Diagnosis*

Chapter 4 *The Hysterectomy*

Chapter 5 *Jumping on the Bed*

Chapter 6 *My New Identity*

Chapter 7 *The Mirror*

Chapter 8 *Calling it Quits*

Chapter 9 *The Roses*

Chapter 10 *God-Sized Dreams*

Chapter 11 *"I am Beauitful"*

Chapter 12 *Follow the Fear*

Chapter 13 *Gratitude*

Chapter 14 *Leveling Up*

Chapter 15 *You Can't Save the World at Midnight*

Chapter 16 *The Next Chapter*

CHAPTER ONE

Pain Changes People

A comfort zone is where dreams go to die. It is where our fears lather up with sunblock and lay in our light until the sun goes out. Where the weeds grow. That's where I think I've been -- in my comfort zone -- sitting here staring at the blank pages.

Through the years, I have started to write this book many times in notebooks, blogs, and emails. I've even scribbled on pieces of paper at 3 a.m., but something's always kept me from finishing it. Now, I think it's time.

One, two, three, four…

I count the steps across my 720 square foot apartment, pacing back and forth and questioning my choices and direction.

Five, six...

"I wish God could sit down and have a talk with me today."

Seven, eight, nine...

"Why are things so hard right now?

Ten... Eleven... Twelve, thirteen, fourteen.

The sound of landscapers cutting the hedges breaks my train of thought.

"I wish I had my own house."

Fifteen, sixteen, seventeen, eighteen, nineteen.

"I can't wait to get myself out of this mess."

Twenty, twenty-one, twenty-two.

"Is there really only 22 steps across my one-bedroom apartment that I have called my 'home' for 12 years?"

I look in the mirror and realize I have been playing offense, defense, and captain of my own cheer squad. I'm just stuck. I have a list of things I want to do and get done, and I am just tired—soul-crushing tired. My tired eyes can't stay open, so I lock my screen and close the laptop.

"Maybe I will just nap for 15 minutes."

The fear of time passing gives me anxiety.

"Fifteen minutes less to do things I need to get done."

My eyelids are heavy, my body becomes horizontal, and I throw the blanket over my legs. My racing thoughts start to slow as I drift to sleep. Even my sleep is restless. I wake up an hour later. I just knew I would sleep longer than 15 minutes. I turn my phone off. It's a quiet rainy Saturday in June, and I feel like I can sit down and write this whole book in 24 hours.

"Why does my mind work like this? "Why is it all or nothing."

I pause to drink some water and watch the blinking cursor on the screen.

"Why would anyone want to read my book? What if it just sucks? What if you are bored already? What if it's too

much sadness for some people to take? What if my dyslexia ruins this, and the publisher laughs at me?"

I quiet my negative thoughts just long enough to remind myself that I am human.

I was listening to an audiobook a few months ago, and it mentioned a theory that was interesting to me.

Stop and look at everything red around the room. Then, name all the yellow things you saw. When you focus on one thing, the other things become less visible. But the yellow things are still there.

I think we tend to do this with a lot of things. We look at the highlight reel of other people's lives -- the beautiful houses people have -- cars, jobs, skills, and looks. We compare our lives to theirs, but our stories aren't meant to be the same.

I've attended many events with motivational speakers where they tell about all the glamour and success they've experienced, but they don't talk about all the shit they went through to get there. When you're in the thick of a hard time, it isn't necessarily inspiring to hear about rainbows and butterflies with no roadmap to get there. You may want to eventually have the things that they have and work hard to get there, but you still have to acknowledge the hardships on your way there. Shitty awful things tend to inspire people to take action, which often results in something better. Maybe that's why I have felt so much self-pressure to get this book done. The one I started writing eight years ago but haven't finished until now because self-doubt kills dreams.

Did you catch the word self-pressure? It is the pressure you put on yourself from carrying all the weight of your own expectations.

Today, I have to set some of the baggage down to knock this book out. Even with all the self-doubt that I may have *(because we all do),* I may inspire people. Maybe thousands, maybe hundreds, or perhaps just one person. I'm sharing the good, the bad, the shitty, then the rainbows and butterflies I've experienced. Yeah, those shitty things – they've happened to me. But I've found that something great always comes afterward.

Maybe my story will inspire you to end bad relationships, call an old friend, or not be a dick to your coworker. Perhaps you will be moved to listen to the woman that says she is fine, even though you know she isn't. Maybe you will be encouraged to start that small business, write the book you have been thinking about, or perhaps be nicer to the people you meet.

I started writing this book long before the words were written down. As I pour my whole heart out with each clicking of the keyboard, I want to take you on a journey through hardship and self-discovery. I hope that it may encourage you never to give up.

Twenty-two steps 12 years ago felt big to me; today, 22 steps seem small. Twelve years ago seems like a lifetime ago. I look back, and it is so different-- yet the same.

I'm still the girl who cheers on everyone with the "go-get-them attitude" and embodies the gentle version of Gary Vaynerchuk's (aka Gary Vee) motto of "Just fucking do it."

First, I'm going to take you back in time a bit, because I believe you have to know where you have been to see where you are going. It will be messy if I start in the middle of my story.

So, I will just start where I remember it all fell apart.

CHAPTER 2

I Was Just Twelve Years Old

My mother always gave us new pajamas on Christmas Eve. My first pair of silk PJs were a deep purple -- a pretty button-down top and shorts. The kind you crawl into bed wearing and squirm around in the sheets to feel the soft-silky feel on your skin.

But this Christmas Eve, when most 12-year-olds are still holding on to the magic of Santa, I laid on the bathroom floor instead, vomiting from the pain of menstrual cramps. That was my first vivid moment of sheer misery. A pain I would become all too familiar with and one I couldn't outrun if I tried. I remember taking seven Advil and probably several Midol that day, but it didn't help.

"It's just cramps," everyone said to me. "It happens sometimes."

The days to follow were filled with handfuls of pain meds to take the edge off. Going to school was terrifying. I could not make it through a class without going to the bathroom, and I wore the pain on my face. Layers upon layers of makeup hid my sunken eyes and dark circles. Then, I went home and laid in pain.

School was already difficult for me, as I was bullied, and I had dyslexia. I was always behind. The only classes I liked going to were the ones my crush was in, because I could at least look at him. *He was dreamy.* I enjoyed art class, but I was even failing that. I had aspirations to be an artist, but my art teacher once said, "You will never be an artist; try a different avenue." *(We will get back to that later…)*

When you're sitting in middle school praying that you aren't bleeding out through the pad you just changed an hour ago, it doesn't help you focus much.

"This is normal. Period pain is normal," was the only feedback I was getting.

My mother had horrible periods, too, and had a complete hysterectomy. She felt helpless because there was nothing she could do for me either. Little did I know, it was *not normal.*

The seven-day flows turned into 10 and 14 days sometimes. I became more and more tired. Bruises covered my body, and I was sleeping every chance I got. As I got older, between tennis practice, running track, and working at an ice cream shop -- every date on the calendar made me nervous. Knowing *that week,* I would be miserable; and no one would know why…

"Oh, you have cramps? Run harder," my coach told me while laughing. I remember being so upset because he thought I was lazy or weak. *(What a dick.)* However, there was a monster inside that just hadn't shown its true colors, and I never wanted it to. But it did.

In the fall of my senior year, I was playing tennis. I loved tennis. One early morning, I had just finished a match with a friend and felt "off." I drove up to the ice cream shop I worked at to get something to eat. I remember feeling dizzy and everything turning a bit blurry.

"Surely, I just needed something to eat?"

I grabbed a soft pretzel with salt. As I stood there talking to someone, I felt like I would be sick. I hopped in my car and headed toward home.

As I turned the corner in the small town of Sunbury, Ohio, my car rolled into a church parking lot. My friend that I happened to be playing tennis with passed by and saw my car. She pulled up next to me and found me in and out of consciousness. I had passed out while driving. She got an ambulance to take me to the emergency room and found out that my first ovarian cyst had ruptured. I was just 17 years old.

My health continued to decline through my senior year.

A few months later after I graduated high school, my parents decided to do a trial separation, my sister got married, we moved out of the house we lived in for 13 years, and I headed off to college.

The second week of college is when 9/11 happened. That changed the world as we knew it. It was a lot to take in.

Meanwhile, the doctor appointments remained abundant, and I remember just wanting to sleep. The pills and pokes made me feel like a pincushion—headaches, bowel issues, vomiting, swollen joints, fatigue, excessive crying, and bruises. I was tested for just about everything under the sun. I even had a bone marrow biopsy to rule out a list of things. I covered my sunken eyes with dark eye shadow.

"You have an unexplained low white blood count; we don't know why," the doctors told me. "You have had so much happen; you are just depressed."

The list of excuses the doctors gave me went on and on, and every single time I left crying and hopeless.

I knew what I was experiencing was just not normal. At this point, it was the fall of 2001. The internet wasn't a thing people had at their fingertips. You couldn't just get on WebMD and type in symptoms. Google had been around, but nothing like it is today.

So, we just had to trust the doctors. We went where our insurance told us to go. I was on a first-name basis with the nurses in the emergency room. When I returned to the emergency room for yet another visit, one male nurse who had helped me before came in and said, "*You again? They haven't fixed you yet?*" as he attempted to get my IV in after several other nurses failed to succeed.

As the years passed, I lost count of the endless trips to the emergency room and the dozens of ruptured ovarian cysts. I went to numerous ultrasound appointments. My fiancé at the time would try and make jokes to calm me. Meanwhile, I was diagnosed with chronic fatigue syndrome by my family doctor. I was put on birth control and anti-depressants. Every time I took the medicine, I got sicker and sicker. I did not believe I had chronic fatigue syndrome *(and later found out that I didn't),* and the birth control pills made me feel like I was on the verge of death with awful side effects.

Eventually, my wedding was called off; friendships ended, I gained weight, and switched between several jobs. The one job I managed to stay at was on a limited schedule, because I was sleeping all the time. I felt trapped in my mind because I didn't feel depressed. Inside I felt hap and wanted my body to be healthy. I just wanted answers, and I had none. I was doing research on my own with no resolution. Even my dad would come home with printed-out pages from the library trying to find answers for me. Meanwhile, I experienced more cysts and more excruciating periods. I kept switching doctors, hoping someone would give me an answer.

I had just turned 25, and once again was trying a new doctor after my latest trip to the emergency room. I was hoping this new doctor would be different than the rest. After a very painful exam, she handed me a pamphlet.

"You have Endometriosis."

Endometriosis
en·do·me·tri·o·sis
/ˌendōˌmētrēˈōsəs/

A disorder in which tissue that lines the uterus grows outside the uterus. The tissue can be found on the ovaries, fallopian tubes, or intestines with endometriosis. It can also be found in the lungs and the brain in some cases.

The most common symptoms are pain and menstrual irregularities. Symptoms include but are not limited to lower abdomen pain, lower back pain, pelvis, rectum, or vagina pain. Painful sexual intercourse or pain while defecating. Abnormal menstruation, heavy menstruation, irregular menstruation, painful menstruation, and spotting between menstruation.

Other gastrointestinal problems can include diarrhea, constipation, nausea, abdominal fullness, and cramping. It can cause chronic pain, heavy or irregular periods.

Some people also report weight gain, bloating, and feeling the need to urinate urgently, and more frequent urination.

Endometriosis is the leading cause of infertility.

1 in 10 women suffers from endometriosis worldwide.

There currently is no cure.

CHAPTER 3

The Diagnosis

I climbed into my little white two-door Honda Civic as tears ran down my cheeks.

"Does this mean I can't have kids?"

I could barely pronounce endometriosis, let alone spell it. I went home to log into the internet to search what endometriosis was and if I could Google a cure. I went into the depths of online pages looking for answers. Maybe somewhere someone had some particular home remedy, perhaps a holistic approach, some treatment I had not heard about.

In the late-night hours, the light from my computer screen would illuminate my face as my dog, Lexie, sat by my side. She was a nine-pound Shih Tzu, and she was like a teddy bear with soft fur that was salt and pepper in color. Her head rest on my leg as my body felt numb and the tears streamed down my face.

"Infertility."

"Working women's disease."

"Painful Periods."

"Incurable."

"Noncancerous disease that spreads."

I felt terrified. I wanted kids. All I ever wanted was to be a mom, but each click made me more confused, angry, and frustrated. There are no treatments; there's no help. Birth control and surgeries to remove reproductive organs filled the pages online.

"What kind of life is this? Was this going to be my life? This is my life."

I already had been living with misery since I was 12. Now, the pain just had a name. At this time in my life, my friends were getting married, having babies, and locking in their first grown-up jobs. I felt left behind -- in everything. Friendships came and went; romantic relationships failed. I barely wanted someone to hold my hand because my whole body hurt.

"I will see if I can," was my standard response to making plans, and those plans often ended up canceled due to the pain I was experiencing.

Facial hair, stomach aches, acne, mood swings, and sleepless nights. Crying. Oh, so much crying. Doctor visits and hopeless responses. Each month seemed to get worse and worse. I was screaming inside, and no one heard a word. My friends did not understand why I never felt well.

"You look fine," friends said. "At least it isn't cancer."

After they said that to me, I remember telling someone, "Well, at least with cancer, you are either cured or die."

I was just miserable. Having sex was painful. I just stopped trying to have relationships. I spent a lot of time with myself, often just sleeping.

At 25 years old, I lived in my parents' house because medical bills kept me from affording my own place. One summer afternoon in June, I was out in their backyard lying in a hammock wishing for a better life. If I close my eyes, I can still vividly see how the sun shone through the trees and I felt the warmth on my face. It was then that I decided I wanted to do photography as a business.

However, the support was not so great. While social media didn't exist at the time, people didn't hold back their opinions in person.

"You need insurance," people said. "Your dyslexia is going to make it hard."

I wanted more to life than trying to make it through each day and going to countless doctor appointments.

I am exhausted remembering all the difficult times as I type.

I had a part-time photography business that I was promoting on MySpace *(I wonder how Tom is doing?)* and was working other jobs – yet, I still was just getting by. Every month it was a cycle – literally. I was back in the hospital with another giant cyst. This was also around the same time when the opioid crisis started coming to light, and hospitals treated everyone as a pill seeker. But I didn't like pills. They made me feel worse.

I started hanging out at bars for happy hour because it took some of the edge off of the sharp pain. I gained weight. *A lot of weight.* I was the heaviest I had ever been and the saddest I had ever been. Meanwhile, life was still happening all around me. I felt like I was standing in a crowded room, completely and utterly alone.

I would get invited to baby showers. I would be so excited each time and make baby blankets, hoping to experience the same thing one day. Jobs would come and go. Still, more trips to the emergency room.

I woke up one day and thought, *"This is enough. This is not the life I want."*

I got up and threw all my medication away.

I moved to the city and got a place of my own. Even that was eventful, I was in a car accident the day I moved, but we will skip that story for another time. I started to feel hopeful, and I lost 100 pounds in a year. I was trying to push through the pain. It only seemed to get worse, which

I didn't even know was possible.

I met someone new and tried to hide how much endometriosis consumed my life so it wouldn't ruin the relationship. I had finally fallen in love again since my wedding was called off five years prior. I remember one night he made me a lovely meal, and I couldn't even eat. I was so sick, and he just didn't understand why. I couldn't hide it and had to tell him. I was missing more and more work, and the ultrasounds were happening every other month. I was buried in medical debt.

Here I was at 29, seeing my eighth OBGYN. I sat in her office as she read the results from my latest trip to the emergency room.

"You have a cyst," the doctor said "We just need to keep an eye on it."

I choked back tears and said, *"Can you go in and just take my left ovary?"*

She looked at me as if I had 10 heads and told her that unicorns were real.

She said, "Normal people don't ask to have their organs removed. Plus, you said you wanted kids, so we will never remove your reproductive organs."

She wrote me a script for anti-depressants, which I never filled -- because I wasn't depressed. I was surrounded by doctors that weren't listening. She had me schedule a follow-up for another ultrasound.

I returned to work, sat down at my desk, and got a "ping." Pings were instant messages that popped up in the interoffice. It was a coworker, and he had asked why I was crying and if I was okay. I told him what had happened, and he sent me a doctor's number that his wife went to.

I picked up the phone: "I know this will sound weird, but I am exhausted. I want to talk to a doctor in an office. Not under some thin sheet half-naked. I want to have a conversation about my health because no one is taking me seriously, and I am miserable. I was just in the emergency room, and my current doctor dismissed my concerns."

The voice on the other end of the phone said, "No problem."

I had an appointment for the following week.

I walked into the doctor's office. The tall man with the deep voice was slightly intimidating. A brown desk separated us. I pulled out three pieces of drawing paper that I had taped together with a timeline of all the events going back to the 12-year-old girl lying on the bathroom floor. He carefully read each line, stopping to ask some questions and then returning to reading. His fingers traced the timeline. Then he crossed his arms, raised his hand to his face in disbelief, and said, "How has no one ever helped you?!"

Tears streamed down my face, but they were much more hopeful tears this time.

I canceled my follow-up appointment with my other doctor and never went back. Nine doctors in 13 years, and I was finally taken seriously.

Two weeks later, days before Father's Day, I headed in to have a laparoscopy to remove my left ovary. I checked in; a nurse handed me a permanent marker, a plastic bag, a gown, socks and a urine cup. I knew what everything was except the marker.

"What's the marker for?" I asked.

"You have to write 'YES' on the side of the ovary we are taking today," replied the nurse.

"Well, that's different."

I switched into the gown with my stomach at my throat, slipped the socks on, and wrote "YES" over my left ovary.

He removed my left ovary and a chocolate cyst (a cyst full of blood) that would have never left my body on its own. My left tube had been twisted, and my ovary was tucked behind my uterus and adhered to my bowels, and covered with endometriosis and lesions. It was probably that way for several years.

He officially diagnosed me with Stage 4 endometriosis. The worst stage.

While I was recovering, the doctor's office I previously was a patient at called and asked when I was rescheduling the ultrasound for my left ovary. (The ovary the doctor didn't want to remove – *that I just had removed.*)

I laughed and said, *"Never; a better doctor chose to listen and help me."*

After one of my ovaries and tube was removed, I felt so much better. I had been out with friends; I went sky diving. I was trying to enjoy life for once. I had been miserable for 12 years. I felt like, for the first time, I could live. I wanted to make up for lost time and was full of energy. Even with the aches in my pelvic area, I was still feeling better than I had ever been feeling. I started working out again and running. I even went on a few dates.

Several months passed and a lot of skipped periods. At the end of September, I went outside to have lunch with some of my friends. While I was there, the first period after surgery began. I felt raw. My insides were trying to escape through my mouth, and I lay in the grass, trying to breathe deeply as pain shot down my legs. The pain meds kicked in and I went back into work, powering through until I could get home to go to bed.

Then, in early October, things took a turn for the worst. The day is imprinted in my mind vividly for many reasons. I was dressed in a white top and black pencil skirt, hair curled just below my shoulders and wearing three-inch heels. I stood next to my mother and my father while we shook hands with people giving condolences for the loss of my grandfather. Mid-conversation with visitors, I hunched over. I felt like someone stabbed me, and I thought, "*Here we go again.*" My mom grabbed my wrist and helped hold me up. I dug deep and pushed through.

The pain came back with a vengeance. I thought I couldn't handle the pain before, but I couldn't function now. Every step I took, every breath I breathed -- I felt horrible pain. An ultrasound determined I had a very large ovarian cyst. Things were much worse than before, *much worse.*

The cyst was slowly leaking. I had a list of things I had to make sure didn't happen, and my doctor gave me an after-hours number to call if things took a turn for the worse. We didn't want an emergency hysterectomy, but we prepared for one. I just wanted to hold out just a little bit longer in hopes of having kids. I was only 29…

That December, my doctor and I brainstormed what we could do to keep my reproductive organs. We had exhausted all options. I had developed horrible side effects from the birth control pills previously. We avoided other treatments that I didn't qualify for because of health issues. In the end, we decided I was going to try birth control pills one last time.

"Maybe these horrible side effects weren't as bad as never being a mom?"

Within a few days, I didn't feel right. I felt sluggish and was gaining weight rapidly. I was sleeping much more and felt very disconnected.

I decided to have a Christmas party in my apartment for something to look forward to. I decorated it with twinkling white lights and hand-painted glitter-coated soup cans with twine and tea lights. The night was so fun. It was the most people I had ever fit in my tiny one-bedroom apartment. We did a gift exchange, ate cookies, listened to Christmas music and shared laughter.

About an hour after they left, I felt sick and my head was foggy. Tears streamed down my face, and I had no desire to live. I knew it wasn't me, I knew I wanted to live. I had so much fight in me that I had to quiet the voice inside my head, and I called and left a message for my doctor:

"Hey, it's me. If you could call me back, I would appreciate it. I am not going to hurt myself, but I am having suicidal thoughts. I know it's the birth control, and I don't want to make it worse by stopping abruptly."

That Sunday, I laid in bed all day with my dog by my side. My phone rang on Monday at 7:02 a.m. when the nurse returned my call.

"Are you okay?" she asked.

"Hey, yes, I am okay," I said.

After we talked for a few minutes, she agreed it was the side effect of the birth control. She agreed as it is a possible side effect that many women don't even know about. The doctor had me stop the birth control pills immediately.

As my period started. I knew the toxic hormones from the birth control were leaving my body. Most of the side effects started fading through the day. The birth control pills were the last-ditch effort to save my reproductive organs. I had held on as long as I could.

It was a warm April day. I was turning 30. I had about 50 people at my birthday gathering. Everyone was laughing and having fun, and I couldn't wait for it to be over. I felt so sick. Dizzy, nauseous, and in pain, I made the most of it. I knew the days with my reproductive organs were numbered. I had hoped I could hold on, be a mother, and not be put into menopause, but it looked bleak.

Soon it was May, and I called my mother at 2 a.m.

"I can't move; the pain is so bad," I said as I had tears streaming down my face. "My stomach is so swollen. It is hard, and it just hurts so bad."

My mother was in Florida taking care of her mother's home. Her mom had passed away a couple of months prior. There was nothing my mom could do from there.

"If I can make it to my pain pills, I can get some sleep and call the doctor tomorrow," I told my mom.

My mom disagreed with my plan but stayed on the phone with me as I attempted to make it across the room to get a pain pill.

"Joslyn, I am giving you 15 minutes," she said on the other end of the line as tears were streaming down my face. "If you aren't even a little better, I am calling 911!"

I didn't want to go to the emergency room. They just told me the same thing repeatedly, and I just would get another costly medical bill. I finally got settled down a bit. At 3 a.m., I got off the phone with my mother after promising to call my doctor in the morning.

The doctor got me in at 3 p.m. As he did an ultrasound, his jaw dropped. He quickly rotated the screen towards me. He was in disbelief. I had fluid and internal bleeding.

He paused.

"And you only took one pain pill 12 hours ago and drove yourself here?!" he asked, shocked. I was fighting a battle with my own body. It was as if I had barbed wire shoved inside my pelvic cavity, and it stabbed me with every breath I took.

A few weeks later, on what would have been my grandfather's birthday-- the one that had passed in the fall.

I put a brave face on and walked into the office and signed on the dotted line.

I was going to have a complete hysterectomy.

CHAPTER 4

The Hysterectomy

Earlier that year, in January, I walked into work and sat across from a colleague.

He said: "You have a look on your face like you have something to say."

"I had the most vivid dream last night!" I said.

He and I were very close; he was kind and looked after me at work. He was easy to talk to, and we knew a lot about each other as we sat watching the clock each passing day until we could leave our 4x4 cubical.

He asked, "Oh yeah, about what?"

"I don't know exactly, but it was about June 6th," I said as I flipped through the pages of my calendar from January to

June. I jotted down: "You had a dream about today," on the square of the 6th.

"I felt so much peace in the dream, and I had no pain and was so happy," I said. "I knew it was June 6th. Everything was beautiful, nothing hurt, and I woke up." In the days leading up to my surgery, I got my last will and testament prepared. I wrote letters to all my loved ones in case something went wrong. One night in the dark, I remember sitting on the floor trying to visualize a life without pain. But I also started thinking about what *life without bringing a child into this world would look like.*

"Was I making the right choice? Did I even have a choice anymore?"

There is no going back from this.

"How was menopause at 30 going to be? Would anyone love me like this? What would a life without pain feel like? What would I do with that time?"

Why was the thought of knowing I would feel good also so terrifying? I did not know any different. I had not known life without pain for so long…

It was a Friday morning at the beginning of June, it was warm outside, and I had to get up well before sunrise. Just washing my face that morning felt like a task. I got in my parents' car and held back my tears as my nerves were getting the best of me as they drove me to the hospital to get a hysterectomy.

I had thought about things so much, yet I still had no idea what to expect.

A young male nurse walked into a room and asked me to take a pregnancy test. He was so casual about it. Like he was taking an order at the drive-thru.

Shocked, I swallowed the lump in my throat and asked, "Why?"

"They have to have it documented before surgery that you aren't pregnant," he said.

As I choked back tears, I realized I would never have to take a pregnancy test again. I felt like I was leaving my body as I hopped off the table to head into the bathroom. When I came back in, my excellent doctor walked into the room. It was quiet. It was the first surgery of the day, so the staff was just getting in, and not all the lights were on throughout the building yet.

I am not one to get nervous typically. But I was this day. I also tend to crack inappropriate jokes in times like these. He said he had to go over a few things with me, and things turned serious. He said I had to tell him what I was having done to make sure I was of sound mind and body. Just remembering that moment pierces my core.

"You are taking my ovary (already had the other one removed), a massive cyst, tube, uterus, and cervix," I responded.

A quiet hush went over the room, trying to be a badass, I jokingly said: "…but you're not taking my balls; those are mine to keep."

As laughter broke out, tears filled my eyes as they wheeled me back into the operating room, repeating to myself, *"Nothing hurts; everything is beautiful,"* to calm my nerves. I climbed onto the table and fell asleep to wake up as a completely different woman. It was 3:05 p.m. With heavy eyelids, I found a clock and a get-well balloon floating next to it.

I was laying in the hospital bed looking at the dry erase board with my list of pain medications, nurses' and doctors' names, and the date: June 7. *The day after the date in my dream.* The pain stopped on June 6. My dream was right. I heard the chatter of my friends saying how peaceful I looked as the doctor fed me ice chips. I was too weak to speak. I went back to sleep.

At 3:15 a.m., I woke up as the nurse came in to check my incision.

I asked her, "Why do I hear babies crying?"

"The baby nursery is outside your door," she replied.

I felt a wave of anger and bitterness sweep over me; I can still feel it at times.

In a foggy state, my mind searched for my own words of comfort. All I could think of was why would they put me in the maternity ward, right in front of the nursery, for recovery when I just lost my ability to have children?

I would never get to be there again. My soul felt crushed. Even as I type these words, tears well up in my eyes almost eight years later.

As she examined the seven-inch incision from hip to hip, she said: "You have the flattest stomach of anyone I have ever seen here!"

"I had a hysterectomy, not a baby," I said agitated.

"I am sorry, you didn't get to have kids, did you?" she embarrassedly whispered. She must have seen the sadness on my face.

I felt so broken. I felt so hot. I felt so jolted. I had gone over all the what if's in my mind, but hearing babies cry was not on that list. The life flight helicopter pad was also right outside my window, and it was loud. With that noise and the hot flashes, I couldn't sleep.

I was hot; I was unbearably hot. I had the nurse turn the air cooler, get me a fan and tons of ice. Hot flashes then were no joke.

She said I had a few visitors earlier that day. It was strange I lost a whole day.

I was starving and asked the nurse for my drawing pad and pen my sister had given me. I got some food in me and started drawing. I had 100 thoughts and never felt so alone.

The sounds of newborns crying echoed outside my room and in my mind, and the night was so dark and empty.

My skin felt soft and warm, and my heart monitor beeped anytime I started getting upset. It was the first time in my life though I had zero abdominal pain -- and I had just been cut open.

I asked to get up and walk around. The nurses were a little cautious, but I went slow. I did laps around the floor. I was determined to get the fuck out of there.

"Seven days in here? Not happening!"

My parents came the next day to visit me.

"The doctor said you are lucky you are alive," my parents said. "The cyst was so large and massive it had filled your whole abdominal cavity. They couldn't even see your right ovary. You were bleeding internally, and if you had waited one more day, you wouldn't have made it. He also said that the endometriosis was so bad that you wouldn't ever carry a child to full term, or possibly even be able to conceive a child anyways at this point."

I remember my mom saying with a soft, sad voice.

I wasn't sure what I was supposed to feel. I fought a battle for 13 years, holding on to the hope of having kids one day, but I wouldn't have been able to anyways.

I remember being upset with one of the nurses who kept telling me how I should feel, how my hot flashes would be, how menopause was, and how painful everything would heal. She was negative, and I remember being angry. Yet, this was the first time I felt well -- even with the hot flashes.

By Sunday night, I had passed all the requirements to go home, and I bounced four days early. My friend picked me up in her car that was easy for me to get in and out of, and I walked up the stairs to my sweet little Lexie wagging her tail.

Even four days post-hysterectomy, I felt the best I had in 13 years.

You Will Never Know My Fight

I'll never get to hear your heartbeat across the monitors
as they run a tool across my stretch marks.
I will never get to know what it's like to have your elbow punch me
as you do somersaults in my belly.

I will never get to know the pain of feeling a contraction
or the way your lungs fill with oxygen as I give you life.
I will never know what it's like to look into your eyes
and see my reflection, the way I look into my mother's.

I will never hear you cry as you wait for me to feed you.
You'll never know the lullabies I'd sing you as you close your eyes at night.
Although, when I was a little girl
I have always felt I could never have you-
You'll never know my fight.

The endless days of pain-
the moments that pierced as the pain took my breath away.
The tears I cried as the fears wouldn't hide.
The time that passed slipped through my hands-
the ones that will never get to hold you.

I never tried to have you,
but I fought for you-and now...
I will never get to know you.
- Joslyn Crowl

CHAPTER 5

Jumping on the Bed

It was 1986, and I was in my sister's bedroom. Like any other 3-year-old, I enjoyed jumping on the bed. The '80s-style brown wood headboard had a round ball post on each side. I was jumping on the bed and fell directly into the headboard, my mouth hit the ball of the bedpost head-on. I remember it very clearly - *even a memory at three years old*. The sides of my mouth ripped open, my gums bled, and I remember my dad holding me in his arms at the sink, trying to stop the bleeding as I cried out. It cut my mouth open, and I have scars inside on both sides still to this day. It also set in motion a ball that hasn't stopped rolling.

Because of the force of the impact, my baby teeth became very weak. In second grade, I lost my front teeth all at once. I think it was like nine teeth. I'm not entirely sure, but it was a lot. When my front teeth grew in, they grew in different directions.

The name-calling began. Kids can be ruthless. I would do my best to ignore them.

"Never let them see you cry," the adults told me. My parents taught me to "be the bigger person and just ignore them" and about the golden rule: "Do unto others as you would have done unto you." (Luke 6:31)

I, eventually, was able to get braces put on in eighth grade. It was the day before Thanksgiving. By the following Monday, my teeth were straight.

Yep, you read that right. In a panic, my parents called the orthodontist, and they got me an appointment right away. They discovered my teeth had no solid roots, and I would need work on my mouth as I got older. They had to make room for the teeth now since they moved so quickly.

They put in a palate expander. What is a palate expander? It's a metal device that hooks onto your teeth, crosses over the roof of your mouth, and hooks onto the teeth on the other side. In the middle of the device is a keyhole. Every night I had to turn the key, and the device would expand. Over time, it would widen my jaw. One night as I turned the key, a loud pop happened. Something snapped. Pain shot across my face and the bridge of my nose. I burst into tears. We called the orthodontist, and they assured us that it was normal and my nose was fine. *(Spoiler alert: It wasn't. It deviated my septum and broke my jaw faster than it was intended to.)*

I wore my braces for two years instead of eight. The orthodontist told me I would need dental implants by age 23. It was always fun to wonder if today would be when my teeth would fall out as I bit into the food. *insert sarcasm* I even was featured at the orthodontist, because it was a rare case at the time.

Eventually, I had to start pulling my food apart, put each bite in my mouth, and choose foods I could eat with a fork or spoon. I had to avoid chewing near my front teeth because they were so loose. Eating became very frustrating.

Meanwhile, the name-calling with my nose added insult to injury. Our family genes have a distinctive nose already; it only got worse as my face shape changed thanks to my jaw and teeth moving. The name-calling of *"big bird,"* *"Gosling the ugly duckling,"* and *"you're a witch"* ...the list goes on.

One time, a group of my classmates lined the halls of high school and would duck down and yell out, "You better duck, or she'll hit you with her nose."

I am still thankful cell phones weren't around when I was in school during the late '90s. *(This was also when I started to have extremely heavy, painful periods.)*

At 19, I had a constant sore throat and tonsil issues. My immune system was getting weaker, and I had to have my tonsils removed.

I was engaged and planning a wedding while trying to figure out why I had a low white blood count and painful periods. I was a mess. The dental implants would have to wait.

Days after my 23rd birthday, I went in for my first appointment to have dental implants placed. It was scheduled in multiple phases over several years. They cut my gums up in the first phase and extracted the teeth. Then, they stitched my gums together to heal. Several weeks after they were healed, I had to have surgery with local anesthesia. I had to be wide awake.

Why wide awake, you ask? Because they had to drill in for the spots where they would place the implants. I had to be able to walk down a long hallway to an X-ray room and check to see if they were set correctly. I do not recommend this. Multiple people had to walk on each side of me to ensure I did not trip or fall because I had two 15-inch metal stakes sticking out of my bloody, swollen, and toothless gums. I was like a walrus with the teeth sticking out, except my "teeth" were metal rods. This went on repeatedly for 8 hours until they got it right.

I felt so much pressure and pain across my nose and eyes halfway through. Everything was swelling. They said it was normal… *(Spoiler alert: It wasn't, they had broken my nose.)*

After they cut the gums open, they placed two implants. Then, they stitched the implants in place with the gums over top of them. Over the next few months, my eyes were black and blue. My nose, jaw, and face ached. I kept questioning if my nose was broken. They all assured me it was fine.

It took nine weeks for me to recover from that surgery. Then, I went back to the dentist. The dentist cut the gums around the implants to reveal the inserted implant tops, so they could eventually connect the teeth and bridge. They again let them heal. After wearing false teeth for over a year, a dental bridge/plate was inserted, and I had new teeth.

But it didn't end there…

CHAPTER 6

My New Identity

I promise I am not trying to make this book doom and gloom. Although it does seem a bit like that so far, I felt that way too when I was living it.

While you're getting a glimpse into my story, there's still more to tell *(maybe a future book?)*. Hang tight, we get to the good part soon.

Fast-forward 10 years. At this point, my dental implants were healed. I had been diagnosed with endometriosis and had a completed hysterectomy. My body and my teeth had healed; the two ongoing problems in my life had been *"fixed."* Life should be going so much better now, *right?*

In June of 2014, I was a one-year post-hysterectomy. Things were going great. I had picked up boxing and running more, and adjusted to menopause. I was working out all the time and was in the best shape and health of my life. I felt so happy and was experiencing the longest stretch of time I had ever gone without pain since I was a pre-teen. I wanted to live life to the fullest and make up for all the lost time.

I had picked up my camera and was taking clients again. I left my corporate office job to work in a photography studio that fall.

That's when I started feeling "off." I kept yawning all the time while I was running and was always short of breath. My face started hurting worse. In September, I woke up one day with blood-red eyes and blurry vision. I thought it was probably just a sinus infection, so I took over-the-counter medication.

I became concerned when I started losing vision in my left eye more and more as the weeks went on. My family doctor told me I needed to go to an ENT because he thought I had impacted sinus and a deviated septum.

"When did you break your nose?" the doctor asked.

An MRI revealed that I had a broken nose with a prior deviated septum.

Insert long sigh and blank stare

In my head, I was yelling, *"I fucking knew it!"*

I had two surgeries because the break was blocking my sinus flow, which didn't allow my sinus to drain correctly.

They were going to be risky surgeries and couldn't be done simultaneously. The doctor flushed my sinus and did a reconstruction of the damaged sinus cavities. Within days, my eyes returned to white. After about a week or so, I regained my eyesight.

Because it wasn't a cosmetic surgery but a repair, a lot could go wrong. With my track record, I was nervous. I didn't get a say in how I was going to look after the surgery. I just had to trust the doctor.

It's strange to think how jumping on a bed at three years old, caused decades of hurt and how one small decision changed my life.

The unknown of what I would look like after surgery made me anxious.

Although I wanted to change my nose I had decided to not change it cosmetically because that is how God made me. Now, I had to because of a medical diagnosis: "repair broken nose and deformity." Was listed on my medical chart.

I found the silver lining, God answered a prayer in an extraordinary way.

On that Wednesday morning in February, I looked in the mirror at the face I had known for 32 years and said goodbye to the girl I once knew.

The surgery took a lot longer than they had planned. When I woke up, the cast was already placed. I just had to sit and wait as I healed at home. My face swelled, and my eyes were so black and blue as the bruises drained down my face into my jaw and neck. I looked wrecked! The cast covered the nose, but the bruises were visible throughout my eyes, cheeks, and jawline. They went across the inside of the roof of my mouth and my upper lip, and it was very swollen.

Looking in the mirror and seeing all the pain written on my face felt like symbolism for all the pain I had experienced from the bullying throughout the years. The pain was leaking out.

I was so nervous.

"What if I look worse? What if I hate how I look even more?"

It was another surgery, another paper to sign on the dotted line that your life is in the hands of another doctor that will change you forever -- and you have no say in the result.

"It's a week's recovery time with the cast, four months of intense restrictions, and a complete year to set," said the doctor with the piercing blue eyes. It was a very overwhelming day. To be honest, it was very overwhelming for several weeks. Being at high risk for infection with my low white blood count, I had to stay pretty isolated from everyone throughout the recovery from both surgeries.

To see yourself one way for almost 32 years, and then one day you look in the mirror and it's different – it's unexplainable. It was so uncomfortable.

Recovery was a challenge. Do you know how many times a day you touch your face? Do you know how often you want to feel your face when you can't? I wasn't allowed to hug anyone. I couldn't pull a shirt over my head. I had to put makeup on with an extra-long paintbrush not to have any force on my face. The doctor said to treat my nose like a thin piece of glass for 3 to 6 months.

I never knew a kiss could hurt. I never knew how many times I blew my nose on a regular basis. Plucking eyebrows, rubbing your eyes, or wiping your upper lip were daunting. Drinking from a straw, which I had to do so I didn't hit my nose on the glass, was inconvenient. Being out in the cold hurt. Showering and putting on my shoes was a challenge, because I wasn't allowed to bend forward.

There is so much they tell you before surgery. But, until you experience it, you don't realize how difficult it truly is. The day had come when I could finally get my cast off. The very bubbly nurse pulled the tubes out of my no.

Sigh, wait for this

The nurse pulled the tubes out of my nose and "POP!" I instantly wanted to throw up. I got super dizzy.

"Are you okay?" the nurse asked.

I knew I wasn't. My septum deviated, but we didn't realize it until a few weeks later.

The nurse described how gorgeous my new nose was and handed me a mirror. I wanted to cry, but I wasn't even allowed to do that. It could irritate my sinus, and I wasn't allowed to blow my nose. They even told my family not to

give me any bad news, because I wasn't allowed to get upset.

I was a stranger to myself. *I hated it.* Everyone was gushing over my new look, and I wanted to hide. It was the attention I had never known. They seemed like genuine compliments. I couldn't have prepared for this mentally. Everyone seemed to love how I looked -- *but me.*

I gazed in the mirror at my face that looked so different. The doctor and his staff had warned me, but until your eyes see it -- your mind can't catch up. It's an adjustment. I was not prepared for the backhanded compliments I received.

"Wow, you look so much better now," people said.

"Thank you for that. I know how you feel now." *insert sarcasm*

I just felt so angry. I was being treated so much better.

And it was annoying me...

"All because my nose was different? I am the same girl I always was? Why am I being treated so much better now?"

The guilt, shame, and anger crept in. As my nose started healing, I started going out to more places. My face looked wrecked, but inside I felt even more wrecked.

It was Valentine's Day weekend, and I was spending a night home with my dog, Lexie, when a notification popped up on my phone that my accounts had been revoked at my job...

"Did I just get let go?"

I texted my ex: "I think I just lost my job."

We still spoke from time to time, and I was still in love with him and wanted to be comforted. We met up to grab a drink, and a fellow patron started talking to him as we stood at the bar. The topic of children came up in a discussion, and he said, "When I have kids..."

The sound of his voice faded in my head as my soul cracked in half and the pain crossed my face. I took a drink of whiskey.

My mind went all over the place.

"Guess he really doesn't want to be with me. I can't have kids."

I knew better to be there with him, but I was just the kind of girl that was always full of hope, even when there was none.

The following day I got a call from my boss. She was closing the studio, and I no longer had a job. I wasn't surprised at this point, and I wasn't allowed to cry-- but I didn't even want to. *It felt like I was a punching bag, taking another hit to the gut.*

 struggled for months to adapt to the woman I was getting to know when I looked in the mirror -- adjusting my hairstyle to my new face shape, being unemployed, and searching for a job while trying to heal from this major surgery. The attention I got from people when I was out was so different. It was nice things, though -- people holding the door open, getting asked for my phone number, and people saying hello. I felt visible for the first time, and it was still oddly heartbreaking.

"Have I missed out on all of this just because of my looks?"

I was meeting people I already knew *for the first time.*

One day I ran into someone I had known for years, and they walked by me after I gave a friendly hello. They said hi like I was a stranger and kept walking on.

"Maybe they were in a hurry?"

Then, it happened again with someone else. As I stood talking to someone I knew, I realized they had no idea who I was! The person standing in front of them wasn't the big-nosed girl they remembered. As I didn't want to waste my time explaining myself, I introduced myself as Tiffany.

I knew Joslyn would trigger some thoughts of the girl they used to know, and I didn't want to go into details. It was easier to be someone new than to watch their face look at me in shock and judgment.

I started to feel pretty and be treated as if I was pretty, and I didn't like it. I wanted to be pretty, but so much resentment settled in.

"Why was I only being treated better because I was pretty? Did I miss out on all of this kindness all these years? Was I that ugly before?"

I couldn't work out while I recovered, and I ate my emotions and gained weight. I was hiding behind the weight so I wouldn't be seen.

I was in menopause, in a situation-ship with unrequited love, had a new face, gained weight, and was newly unemployed.

"Is this rock bottom?"

CHAPTER 7

The Mirror

"Of course not; rock bottom has a basement."

I stood on the front lawn of my parents' home. It was built in 1949 by my great-grandparents on two acres out in the country. My father was named after my great-grandfather, who made the house himself. I looked at the old trees on the property and listened to the hum of cars speeding by. At the time, I had a job managing a restaurant and took the day off to help my parents.

It felt like I was standing in the middle of a storm, and it was spinning all around me. My dad put all his tools and gadgets out on the front lawn, along with the unfinished projects he wished to build, but time slipped away from him. My mom carried out her belongings from the house, asking me, "Do you think someone would buy this?"

As I robotically stuck price tags on my parents' belongings. My dad looked defeated and broken. My mom went through the motions, and I just stood there doing my best to be a supportive daughter.

It was early spring, and cars were rolling down the gravel

driveway to check out the garage sale my parents were having because they were losing their house to foreclosure. It was especially tough to see the hurt my parents were experiencing, losing the house that was in our family for generations.

Life happens sometimes, and there is nothing we can do about it. My parents were always hard workers. My father suffered two massive heart attacks when I was in first grade. As I got older, I became sicker, and the medical debt became too much. Like many families, living paycheck to paycheck, our family never got ahead. So, any setbacks were significant setbacks.

When my father was working relentlessly to find a job

after being laid off, months went by without a paycheck. Then a call came that shifted all our lives forever.

My dad's aunt called him.

"You better go check on your dad," she said. "I saw him today, and he was acting differently."

When my dad showed up, my grandfather had already passed away. I remember that day so vividly. The sound of my mother's voice with tears streaming down her face. I was standing and fell to my knees because the weight of my broken heart pulled me down. The weeks and months that followed were so hard. Packing up a house that hadn't been touched since his wife *(my grandmother I never got to meet)* died from complications from an ovarian cyst rupturing when she was in her early 30s.

Then, a few months after my grandfather passed, my mother got a call.

"Mom fell," said my aunt to my mom.

As a few short days went by; my grandmother passed away. Now, my mother was dealing with the loss of her mother, my last living grandparent. Mom was helping pack up her mother's home that they had spent their whole lives in.

Then, my mom got called into a meeting room at her job and was told her position was being eliminated company wide. She only had a week's notice.

Some things in life you just don't recover from. They slipped further behind on the house payments, and then it was too late. Watching my parents sell whatever they could on the lawn that day was hard. Among the things for sale was a tall mirror leaning against the garage. I turned around and thought, *"That girl is so pretty."*

I thought it was someone at the yard sale until I realized *I was the girl in the mirror.* I was shocked to my core. I am unsure if I had ever *felt pretty before.*

It was the first time since surgery that I could really see myself again. I will remember that moment my whole life. My eyes welled up as I felt what everyone kept saying to me. I thought I deserved more. I thought that I could be more. I felt I needed to do more. But a dark cloud and heavy weight sat on my shoulders. The world almost fell hush, and everything around me was slow motion. Then, as the moment broke, the wave and rush went over me. Something inside of me awoke.

I looked back in the mirror, then at my mother, and then over at my dad, and I thought:

"I never want to work for someone else and give that much

power to take my job away to cause a ripple in my life like this."

That week at work, I felt like I was in the wrong place. I watched my coworkers and staff engage with each other and customers, and it all felt utterly pointless. I felt like I had already checked out of the job. I cried every single day, exhausted.

 had fought through so much for my health and life, over six figures of medical debt through the years, trying to create a better business model for my photography business. The fast world of restaurant life was catching up with me. I had only been there for about two months, and it was two months long enough.

My dyslexia took me twice as long to count all the drawers every night at 3 a.m., and I just didn't feel well (assuming it was because of my last two surgeries I was still recovering from). I was exhausted. I hadn't touched my camera in weeks and hadn't worked out either, gaining weight and getting further from my goals.

My family was heartbroken with all of the losses around us -- surgeries, jobs, deaths. We were worn down. Enough was enough. I made a decision that day to put myself first!

To follow my calling.

CHAPTER 8

Calling it Quits

On a Friday evening, I picked up my paycheck for 120 hours. That was two weeks' worth of pay, and it wouldn't even cover rent. I went out with some friends that night. The following day, I called in and quit. (It isn't the most respectable idea to quit on a Saturday in a restaurant, as that is a busy day, but I didn't care. It ended up being the best decision, *but I didn't know it at the time.*)

Then, I slept for hours. I got up, made something to eat, prayed, and went to bed. The following day, God answered a prayer and sent a woman my way for photography services that paid more than the paycheck I was handed two days prior.

I knew I was going to be okay.

"What are you going to do now?" my friends and family asked.

"I am going to be a full-time photographer!" I answered

While I put on a strong face, I would fall asleep worried about how I would pay my bills. I would stack my medical bills into a heap on the counter. I worried about my parents as they moved into an apartment. I was eating crackers and Italian dressing for dinner as I watched YouTube videos on how to become a better photographer and a better business owner.

I had notebooks everywhere and sayings written on the bathroom mirror with dry-erase markers. Vision boards covered a whole wall in my bedroom. I said *"no"* to invites, and some days didn't move from the couch as I was on my computer researching and working all day. I was learning how to market myself better, plan shoots and get all my ducks in a row. I took odd jobs, and I started selling everything I owned -- including the couch in the living room and knives in the kitchen -- until one day I was just sitting on the floor working with nothing around me but my dog, Lexie, on her bed.

One by one, 90 percent of the items around me disappeared. Each time a thing would leave, my apartment would get more empty, and my determination to get stronger and stronger. People were getting more and more

concerned about me, but most were just talking shit about me.

I knew my apartment would have furniture again one day, and it would be even better. I was so proud that I made $4,000 just from selling my belongings for one month. Some items were a bit harder to get rid of. I had a gorgeous black and white photo of trees in the winter. It was a gift my mother had given me for Christmas several years prior. It had happened to be in the car when I was in my car accident and was untouched from all the other damage. The day came; I sold it too.

I trusted the process. I knew each day I would get closer to my goals. I worked hours behind the scenes. You name it, I climbed into the world of a full-time business and laid brick by brick around me. Sometimes things would go amazing, and sometimes it would be a failure.

Failure is a part of success.

I might not have had the resources or funds I needed to go full-time in my business, but I started to eat, sleep, and dream of photography.

Then one day, when I was out with my mother, someone asked what I did for a living. My mother proudly and quickly responded; "She is a photographer."

She was right. It was hard work and determination to get

there, but that is what I was. I was a photographer, and that was what was paying my bills now.

But soon, the universe wanted to add to the stack of medical bills. I was not feeling well, and it was not from my last two surgeries. I ended up back in my not-so-favorite place -- the emergency room. I was going sepsis. Several weeks later, I had my gallbladder removed.

At this point, I needed a punch card for surgeries. *One of them needed to be free at this point, right?* I also ended up with stomach ulcers. The over-the-counter pain pills through the years had caught up to me.

Add in the stress of everything and the weight gain, and my body told me that I wasn't okay.

At this point, I may have started asking, *"God, why me? Why does this bad shit keep happening to me? Why can't I just be healthy? Why can't my business just take off?"*

Thankfully, I slowed down long enough to hear him.

He was making me stronger for a bigger purpose.

Nothing makes you feel more alive than almost dying.

The thing is, when people talk about a near-death experience, it leaves people mystified. You don't understand it until it happens to you.

It is lonely. It is painful. It is quiet.

You think about the people that matter the most to you.

The fact that you didn't put laundry away, you ate a whole carton of ice cream watching a sappy love story, you didn't get the job -- These things don't cross your mind when you are sitting in a hospital bed listening to the beep of the machine as you watch reruns of Golden Girls on TV.

You think of the people who held your hand and the smile of the person you love; you think how soft your dog's fur feels in your hand as you pet them. You think of the most beautiful sky and sunny day. The days become stranger as you get better, because your desire to live is so strong you feel like your soul is pulling you along.

You want to do everything all at once, but you're so tired. So, you do nothing at all.

Recovery causes an idle body but your mind plans.

The things you want to do, the places you want to go, the things you want to accomplish -- You want to do it all at once, but your body is unable to.

I dug deep because at this point… I HAD TO GET BETTER.

"I have too many things I want to be! I have gone through too much shit to give up now! I want to open my photography studio. I want to write a book. I want to inspire others to keep going. I want to do ALL the things, right now!"

I got out of the hospital and started working towards it little by little.

Several years later, things were getting better.

It was the early summer of 2017. The sky was a gorgeous shade of blue, and the clouds were so fluffy white. I had a meeting with someone from an organization I was a member of.

I put on a black button-down shirt; I was known to wear black often. I grabbed a white skirt I had picked up from a thrift shop and slid on my Michael Kors high heels. My hair was curly, and I was feeling fun and flirty.

As I pulled into the parking lot, raindrops started hitting my window and the humidity rose. I enthusiastically knocked on the door and waited for the answer. She let me in, as her young nieces and nephews ran around the room chaotically. I took a seat, and the kids left with their parents. The woman asked me; "What do you want to do with your business?"

It was a straightforward reply for me, as I have always pretty much known what I want. I spend a lot of time with myself, and these things come naturally. "I want to have a photography studio and photograph portraits. I want to write a book and become a motivational speaker."

To me, these all sounded pretty simple and doable. I confidently sat across from her as she shuffled papers on her desk. She then went on to give me her credentials as a recruiter -- as a way to back her words for the next statement she set out to say. She folded her arms and leaned into me from across her desk.

Letting me know her longevity in the field, she was confident in her reply.

"I have been doing this for decades," she said. "If I had someone come in here looking for a job and listed all those things, I wouldn't even look at their resume. I would tell them they are focusing on too much, and they just need to pick one thing and do it. Too many things will cause nothing to get done."

It was thereafter the words she said fell on deaf ears, and I mentally checked out. I sat there staring with a smile on my face.

"This woman is fucking crazy! Who does she think she is? She works as a job recruiter, and this is the advice she is giving? You have got to be kidding. I didn't ask for a job,

and I didn't ask for advice. Why is she going off about this?"

I was there for a meeting about the organization I was a member of. She proceeded to go on about all the things she thought I should be doing and why what I wanted to do was never going to work.

I left shortly after, gripping the steering wheel tightly on the way home, I called my mom, fuming.

"Get what this bitch just said to me," when I got home, I got on my computer, and typed up an email to the board. I decided to quit the organization, I had already had issues with them, and this was the breaking point. I didn't want to be associated with her. I dubbed her the "dream crusher."

I sat there typing away at my email when I realized a fly had flown into my tiny one-bedroom apartment. It was a big fly too, the kind that hummed in flight. It would land in a plant, and I couldn't find it. I tried to save it and get it out, and it would just fly away from me.

I would sit back down, and it would stay quiet and then start up again. I only became more and more irate. I would get up and try again. In between trying to write this email, this fly was just pissing me off. I finally managed to get it to the sliding door, and then it flew back into the apartment. My anger building, I sat back down at my computer.

I began doubting myself.

"Why does everyone feel like I can't be all these things, why can't I photograph people and have a studio? Why can't I write a book? Why can't I be a motivational speaker? Am I not good enough to be any of these?"

Self-doubt crept in, and my head became heavy on my shoulders. The fly returned back to the door, and I was more annoyed.

I got up, no longer in my heels but a colorful pair of capri pajama pants and a T-shirt, and went over to the sliding glass door. Self-doubt was rolling in my head as I struggled to get this damn fly out of my apartment. I opened the screen door and was able to maneuver the fly between the door and the screen, and I stepped outside, shutting the door behind me. Shaking the screen door was causing my curly hair to bounce and my dog was staring at me confused. I just wanted to get the fly to move. I just kept saying to the fly, "Don't give up! You don't know how close you are!"

I was shaking the screen more, my arms tense as I was full of emotion. I rattled the doors so hard and screamed at this fly, "DON'T GIVE UP! YOU DON'T KNOW HOW CLOSE YOU ARE!"

Then, I froze. I realized I wasn't talking to the fly-- but myself. As I stopped, the fly became free and flew away. I was paralyzed with anger, fear, and rejection in a doubt-filled state. I felt misunderstood, broken, and trapped on the inside -- just like that fly.

I stopped crying, gathered myself together, and pulled my head back up. I sent the email to leave the organization and went back to enjoying my day. I realized I had allowed someone that I didn't even know to cause me to doubt myself.

No one should ever have that much power over you. Your dreams are yours, and not everyone is meant to understand them.

One thing I remember from my pre-op appointments before my hysterectomy is telling my doctor about all the things everyone kept telling me about how I was going to feel and what I would experience. He gave me some of the best advice; that no one's stories are the same and they have not been down the road I have. My story won't look like theirs or theirs like mine.

I held onto that advice as I healed after my surgeries.

This life is *your story*. No one will ever know each day of your life and the thoughts and emotions you feel; they do not know what keeps you up at night or makes your soul shine. They don't see the pain you have survived or the darkness you have walked through to get to the light.

Although I share parts of my own story with you, you will truly never know -- just like I won't truly know yours.

Because of this, you should know you can be whoever you want to be, whenever you want to be. When you are trapped in between a glass door and net, and someone tells you that you can't break free, don't give up. You don't know how close you are to being free.

I went on to photograph the most gorgeous set of trees in the fog. That photo looked even better than the gorgeous black and white photo of trees in the winter that I sold off with all my belongings. I opened my photography studio later that year, which I still operate. Now, I also mentor other photographers. I have been hired for events for motivational speaking. Plus, you are reading my book.

That woman from the organization was wrong.

If you have someone in your life telling you that you can't do something you want to do, there is a good chance they are wrong!

"Don't give up! You don't know how close you are!"

CHAPTER 9

The Roses

I started noticing that parts of me were changing, for the better. The fog of pain I had been in for so long was lifting, I was slowing down and enjoying life more.

I started having house plants all over my home.

I found myself talking to them, encouraging them to grow. Then at other times, I was forgetting to water them.

I added it to my to-do list.

"Monday: water plants."

I catch myself often ignoring the task as I become busy.

"I'll get to them later."

Then, something else pulls me in a different direction. I sit down at 11:20 p.m. I look at the clock and exhale. I have nothing left on my to-do list except water the plants. No one needs me; no one is asking me questions. It is peaceful

-- I haven't felt that in months. I go to bed without watering the plants.

Days pass by, the edges of the leaves turn in and hang low. They look defeated, thirsty and weak. I don't talk to them or touch their leaves. I don't make sure they have sunlight or even water.

Without love, water and encouragement, they are dying. They struggle to grow to their full potential. They hang their leaves down, and they don't give off as much oxygen and soon lose their life.

I, too, have felt like a wilted plant. Most likely, you have to, especially if you have ever started a business or fought an illness on your own, especially endometriosis.

We can't put off watering the plants and still expect them to grow. Encouragement, sunlight, love, and lots of water are needed -- daily.

I used to walk into Kroger, a grocery store here in Ohio, and the first thing I did was stop and smell the roses. They have remodeled the store now, and I briefly see the discounted flowers at the self-checkouts.

On this particular day, I ran in for a loaf of carbs – *eh, I mean bread.* I saw a beautiful bouquet of white roses. I was drawn to them, expecting the tag to say $24.99. Instead, it read $3.99.

I instantly pick them up and begin examining them.

"Why are these beautiful roses so cheap? No wilted leaves; no missing petals. I rarely buy myself anything, let alone roses."

I sit them down. Then, I think...

"No, I need to get them. I love white roses, and they can brighten my home."

Then, I started sabotaging myself.

"You don't deserve these; what have you done to deserve these?"

I quickly grabbed them, ignoring the self-hate, and headed to the check-out before I changed my mind for the third time. I return home and placed them in a pale of wa' trying to figure out why something so beautiful and fragrant was so cheap and discarded. I enjoy them for a few hours. Then, I see a stem sticking out.

I pull the stem out and quickly count. Eleven roses. Eleven beautiful roses. They discounted them because one had broken off. It made me sad, not because there weren't 12, but because it was instantly thought to be unworthy and discounted with just 11 roses.

It made me wonder.

"How many times have I done this to myself? How many times have my friends treated themselves like this? How many times have my clients done this to themselves?"

Sometimes we might feel like we're the bouquet missing a rose, and we're not as valuable. However, the right person will see your value, even if you feel like you're missing something.

Buy the roses for yourself. You deserve them, but also remember to water the plants, and take care of yourself...

CHAPTER 10

God-Sized Dream

At this point in my life, I was reasonably healthy. I wasn't sleeping much, and everything was about the hustle and grind.

"Must build my business, hit six figures, be the best, and get all the clients! Must win all the awards! Must get a studio! Must do everything all at once!"

I was 33, and one year into my full-time business, doing it all on my own after a series of unfortunate events. I looked back and realized I had lost an ovary, had a hysterectomy, my parents lost their home, I got a new face, I lost my job and started a business, went septic, and sold everything I owned to build a business with $150 to my name. I was so excited that I had come so far, and on the path God had planned for me.

But the Devil had a hold of my feet, and it felt like I was standing on quicksand.

I cannot even begin to explain how many times my body tried to fail me while I ran my business and struggled to pay medical bills, day-to-day bills, and business expenses. I pressed on through the dozens of surgeries, doctor visits, and life-altering diagnoses. It was nothing short of exhausting.

I once read a quote: "What a sad thing when they call her beautiful and strong, and she still goes to bed alone every night."

I walked this journey by myself. Often times it felt like I was standing in a crowded room yet feeling all alone. I have had the support of so many people, but the pain I have carried behind closed doors many do not know about.

My friend always tells me, *"Nighttime is for sleeping, not for thinking."*

But, that's just when thoughts seem to be the loudest and the worry seems so real. As the day ends, the nervousness only becomes stronger. You know when you wake up the next day, you feel like you need to solve every problem by 9 a.m. It is an exhausting roller coaster trying to live your dream while fighting your own body.

I always want to be the strong one, the one to help, and the one to be there for everyone. The first to the party and the last to leave. I love helping people, I love knowing I made someone smile.

My sister sent me a card years ago that said the famous quote: *"Be the change you wish to see in the world."* - Gandhi

She added a quick note: "This made me think of you."

I feel like a hypocrite when I'm constantly supporting others but don't allow others to support me. Although I am strong, I am also weak.

Questioning if I was on the right path, I went for a walk through the mall. I walked past a store, felt my soul pull me to turn around, and had to go back in. I knew there was something in their God that wanted me to find. I ran my eyes down each shelf as I walked through listening to the music. My heart filled with love, and I felt comforted. I kept looking as if I was following a rainbow to the pot of gold. It was then that I found the book *God-Sized Dream* by Halley Gerth. The teal cover and the skeleton key matched my business brand at the time, and the title was exactly what I was feeling.

I immediately purchased it. As I was reading, it just clicked. I had God-sized dreams for my business -- not just taking photographs but writing books, talking at public events, and teaching photography. Only God knew what else would be in store, and He led me to this book to remind me to focus on the big picture because the events that were about to happen would need me to level up and do a lot of soul searching and thinking.

They say owning a business is one of the hardest things you can do. I come from a long line of entrepreneurs and learned a thing or two along the way. I know ups and downs are normal, but this was a down I won't ever forget. The game-changer of all games for me.

There are a few things that are devastating for a photographer, like a camera malfunctioning, a computer breaking, or a hard drive failing... Losing the memories we work so hard to preserve.

It was just like any other time, I sat down at the computer and plugged in the external hard drive. I selected my folders to transfer over and went on about my work. I came back a few minutes later to realize that my computer was frozen. The computer I worked to the bone, sometimes up to 19 hours a day for years. The computer that survived the water bottle flood of 2017. *(Story for another day.)* The workhorse that, although slow, never let me down -- was frozen.

With my external hard drive plugged in.

With over 40,000 of my files.

With the book (this book) I had been writing.

My personal files, my previous clients' files -- attached to a frozen computer.

I walked away, said a prayer, and came back 30 minutes later. There it sat, still frozen in time. I unhooked the drive and hard drive from the computer as the pit of my stomach ached and my fingers felt frozen. The laptop slowly turned back on. It appeared to be working just fine, slower than usual, but it turned on.

I plugged the external hard drive back in to take a look.

I waited.

Then, a clicking started, like a broken record trying to find the rhythm. It clicked and clicked and clicked.

My heart sank further.

I walked away.

"This is not happening right now. Not all my files!"

Thankfully, I kept all my clients' orders differently, and no one was going to be delayed. But all my backups... my book *(This book I had been writing)* and all my files were gone.

My heart sank even more, and everything felt numb as I remembered a story my mentor had told us before. A multimillion-dollar photographer with over 25 years of experience lost seven hard drives.

"We're human; it happens. She survived; I will survive!"

Two hours passed of pure shock.

"This is real. This is happening. Figure it out."

I called my friend, and we went to get margaritas and tacos. It's the only logical thing to do when your entire career and all you have to show for it is erased. Who needs a salt rim when tears are flowing anyways?

The following day, I drove into a shop in Sunbury, Ohio, and had them look at the hard drive, and they labeled it as a *"critical failure."* That is precisely how I felt. *Like a failure.*

Everything I was so proud of was gone -- the hard work and the sleepless nights, the art I created, and the moments in time I froze with a shutter click. I felt shattered. As I sat in my car and prayed for strength, I felt a hush.

I made a few calls to my business insurance and my lawyers, and the verdict came back. Since I had no open client orders, the data retrieval wouldn't be covered. It would cost me a minimum of $2,000 to get them back.

I needed those photos for marketing, social media posts, websites, and ads. Needed a new computer and a new external hard drive. I had nothing to do any of that.

I spent the next few days with friends and family. I walked away from work and enjoyed floating on a raft that looked like a donut on Alum Creek, a local lake, joining friends with boats, and relaxing on the water. I ate chocolate and binge-watched *Friends* on Netflix. I regrouped. I prayed.

I debated walking away from my business altogether. The computer was done for; I just couldn't trust it. The files were gone for now, and I needed thousands of dollars to replace the computer. I felt humbled and terrified all at the same time.

I am such a prideful person. I work so hard for all that I have and put my full effort into everything I do. A technical malfunction left me questioning my life choices and talents.

I got a plan of action together and put it into motion. My body was telling me to give up and walk away, but God was up to something when I was down.

A ladder appeared in the basement of rock bottom I had been hanging out in, and I started to climb out.

A month later, I ended up with a new computer and a new look for my business. I had the biggest month of sales in my business in nine years. Four months later, I opened my first photography studio.

My studio was fully booked up and was crushing goals!

My body had changed for the better, my face changed for the better, and now my mind was finally starting to.

CHAPTER 11

"You Are Beauitful"

It was a chilly January evening, and I had been working tirelessly on my new studio. The prior November, I signed a lease for the long-awaited space, and the grand opening was quickly approaching. My to-do list was getting shorter, but the tasks were more difficult and time time-consuming. If I wasn't working at the studio, I was working away on the computer between sessions and bookings

Life seemed so different, and I was finally starting to get some furniture for my apartment again.

When I started down the journey of being a full-time business owner, I started listing to every "self-help, law of attraction, money-making, change yourself for-the-better" book and podcast. The most significant takeaways were gratitude, prayer, and affirmations. They are game changers.

I am big on affirmations. I believe what we put out into the universe; we get back. I game-changers doing them in high school after watching the movie *The Secret*. I didn't tune into it much until becoming a business owner and listening to fellow motivational speakers. Then, it all started clicking.

"I am" is a very powerful phrase, and I wanted to add that to my client experience. So, I sat down and designed a simple bookmark that read:

"I am beautiful."

It included my name and contact information on the back. *Genius right?* They can look at it every day. They have my info if they ever decide to book a shoot. They would look at it and truly believe and know they ARE BEAUTIFUL.

I designed them in Photoshop and quickly sent them off to a printer. They arrived the week of my grand opening, and I put them with my business cards on the tables.

Grand opening day arrived. It seemed so surreal. I put on my favorite Michael Kors dress and blew up some black and silver balloons. I put out a guest book next to all the album samples and photographs hung on the wall -- name on the front door.

Past clients stood holding the bookmark next to their portraits on the wall. Everyone loved them. They were a huge hit.

I hired a photographer to shoot the event. I was on cloud nine. It was finally happening for me!

A few days later… *yes, days…* later.

I received a message letting me know that there was a spelling error.

*"I am **beauitful**."*

I quickly leaped up and shuffled to get the business bookmark, my heart beating fast. I realized my dyslexia had struck again.

Publicly all over my business. On one of the most important days of my life.

This wasn't the only catastrophe.

The photographer that came to capture the event had ruined all my photos, and I had no professional photographs of my very first studio's grand opening.

At this point in my life, all I could think was, "If I didn't have bad luck, I'd have no luck at all."

I made a Facebook post speaking about dyslexia and sharing some of my story.

In fifth grade, I was finally diagnosed with dyslexia and labeled as "LD" (Learning-disabled.) I had struggled with reading and would have to sit for hours reading into a tape recorder and then listen to it back. A lot of testing after testing trying to figure out why I was struggling in school.

People thought I wasn't trying, that I just wasn't smart and that I was just being lazy. I went to a center for testing that said I had a comprehension level of a 12th grader, but my reading level was at that of a first-grader. You can understand everything, but you just can't read it correctly because of your own mind.

"How did I pass five grades before someone helped me?"

I skimmed through school, taking every art, music, and computer class I possibly could. I avoided reading and math like a hospital during flu season.

As I got into high school, it became more challenging to focus on things. I was just done. I was getting by with C's and B's but had to take some credits to graduate. I took an art class and got a D, and she told me I would never be an artist.

"Never be an artist?"

That was all I had going for me. I hated school; I found myself writing in my free time to escape reality.

Enjoying speech class, I was encouraged to take an English class. It didn't hurt that my crush was in that class, too. I ended up dropping out of English class, but the teacher left an impression on me as they discovered I loved to write. I became a teacher's aide during study hall. They encouraged me to write and would read over my love notes and poems.

I mostly kept my writing to myself, because my dyslexia was so awful. I was 23 when someone read something I wrote and I heard positive feedback for the first time, other than from a teacher. I started sharing a little more, and a little more. Then, social media came around with an option for "notes." I decided to post a story I had written about red lights.

I sadly don't have the story anymore. It went along the lines of how getting stopped at red lights can change the whole course of your day, and even your life. How every action has a reaction. But the meaning got lost as I was publicly humiliated by friends and family belittling me and my spelling.

Another point for dyslexia.

I stopped sharing my stories publicly.

The thing about dyslexia is that no matter how many times you re-read something, your eyes physically don't see the mistake.

When I went full-time with my business, I was worried about my dyslexia. I was constantly second-guessing myself with social media posts, newsletters, and emails. I would hit send and then read the email another dozen times. I'd even go back and read it again in the middle of the night after sending it. I felt like a hamster running on a wheel. I even knew I wanted to write a book, but how could I do that when my dyslexia was always front and center?

Then months later, I was out running and my phone dinged. I looked down and had a message from a friend. It was a screenshot and a sweet message telling me: *"Don't let this get to you."*

Someone had my misspelled bookmark card and was publicly shaming me and my business on a public forum. "This is supposed to be a business owner, and they can't even spell 'beautiful' right," the post said.

"For fuck's sake! Can I catch a break?"

Defeated. I felt so defeated.

My fears around dyslexia were staring me in the face. I had nowhere to hide or go.

Mind you, I was on the side of a busy road during my run when I got the message. I was so mad and sad, and I still had to walk back home.

"What if this ruins me? What if potential clients don't choose me as a photographer, because I spelled 'beautiful' wrong?"

I walked five miles that day, teary-eyed most of the way. I was over this crying bullshit. I got home, took a deep breath, and opened my phone.

I sent the guy who made the post a message *thanking* him for advertising for me and expressed that dyslexia is not something to be made fun of and is protected by the Americans with Disabilities Act. He never responded but did remove it.

The support of my friends on Facebook was terrific.

People even contacted his job he was a manager at about how upset they were over him making fun of someone with ᵃexia. *They were pissed, to say the least...*

Never underestimate the power of supportive people!

"It's great," a fellow business owner told me. "It shows that even with imperfection, were still beautiful."

I have learned that seeing words backward makes me one hell of a photographer because I see things differently. If I didn't have dyslexia, I wouldn't be where I am today.

It took me a long time to see it but, Dyslexia is a gift. Did you know that 1 billion people have dyslexia and 35 percent of entrepreneurs are known to have dyslexia?

I sometimes think about what my life would be like if I had never leaped into my business because I spelled words wrong/backward from time to time.

How many lives would I not have touched?

How many people would I not have told that they are

beautiful, no matter how it is spelled?

What if I would have let this fear stop me from going after my dreams?

CHAPTER 12

Follow the Fear

Someone asked me a few years ago what I was afraid of, and I quickly responded: "Nothing."

I thought I had no fears. I had faced the war zone in my mind and looked death in the face. What was I to be afraid of now?

I was so wrong…

When I went full-time with my photography business, I had NO idea how much I would change. I had no idea the new dreams and visions that would come to me, the soul-searching and life-cleansing things I'd do.

Things that happened to me as a child significantly impacted me and subconsciously left me a mess. As I got deeper into following my mentor and listening to other motivational speakers, I realized I had some work to do. The demons often sneak in over and over again.

"What are you afraid of?" I asked myself.

Fear of *"What if they don't like me?"* Fear of *"What if I get sick again?"* or *"What if my dyslexia shows?"*

Fear of being wealthy. Fear of not being good enough.

Fear of not being pretty enough. Fear of not being skinny enough. Fear of asking simple questions. Fear of talking on the phone. Fear ruled all.

Then one day, I heard this statement: *"Follow the fear..."*

What a jolt.

The fear was getting my focus. It mostly leads back to childhood where the bullying was often and the illnesses, I was battling were daunting. Survival mode was on autopilot.

When I got into my 20s, I cut dozens of friends and family out of my life. We were taught at a young age to forgive but were never taught to cut toxic people out of our lives or to stand up for ourselves.

The damage was already done though. As I set out to become successful and to achieve these in my early 30s -- wanting to make six figures, write a book, have my dream home, own a gorgeous photography studio, get married, and have a family -- I sat in the dark remembering those voices I heard decades ago.

"I'm not good enough."

Sometimes it's a daily occurrence to tell the voices that give me a million excuses as to why I can't to *fuck off* and get out of my way! I have dreams to achieve!

But just like you, I have demons too. I'll be damned if they stop me from being who I am meant to be. Maybe it's the anger still; perhaps it is the fear that keeps me going.

"Prove them all wrong."

I was listening to a podcast where they talked about the people in your life and on your social media. They said to treat social media like your home. Who you have in your life and newsfeed should respect your house.

Cut people out of your life if they don't support you, love you, praise you, laugh with you, believe in you, and respect you. Be around those that lift you up. You are enough.

Yet, I sat pondering all the fears I had.

"What if no wants me to photograph them? What if I can't pay for a studio? What if no one will read the book I want to write? ...But what if they do?"

Even now, writing this book with a publishing deadline, I still question if this will inspire someone to not give up. I remember in elementary school; I carried a green plastic briefcase that my dad had picked up at a local thrift shop. (Still to this day, he tells me about all the deals he finds.)

I filled that briefcase and took it everywhere I went. It was filled with colored pencils, crayons, and paper. It was filled with drawings of how I wanted my dream house to look one day, as I wanted to be an architect. As I got older, I wanted to own a greeting card company. I had always wanted to be an entrepreneur. I wanted more out of life than I had. I wore my heart on my sleeve, and many people had a tendency to hurt me. Life was filled with many disappointments, losses, and strange life circumstances.

As I sit here, I remember that little girl who wanted to change people's lives, even if it was just her own.

If you would have told that little girl that she would grow up and have new teeth, a new nose, not able to have children, have a constant struggle with dyslexia, almost die, have 17 surgeries, and a long list of other things... She wouldn't have believed you.

She wouldn't have wanted to move forward in life. But what if you said to that little girl that she could grow up and be whatever she wanted to be?

Her friends, and even her own family, might not have believed in her, but something inside of her told her that she could write a book, own a business and inspire others.

Sometimes it is hard to believe that good is coming when you're in the middle of a storm. The complicated things in life *had to happen* to transform you. Owning my own business has been the most difficult, and the most rewarding thing I have ever experienced.

What is holding you back? What is your fear?

CHAPTER 13

Gratitude

I sat with my head in my hands. The silence was deafening.

Life had swallowed me whole and finally broke me. Grief.

"Grief will demand to be felt." I once heard the phrase in the movie *The Fault in Our Stars*. I was feeling every inch of it.

Grief has its own overwhelming sense of entitlement. It picks what you are doing that day. It is like a stubborn couple that won't speak to each other. Your body does one thing while your head does the other. You weigh the exact same as the day someone you loved died, but now you feel the weight of 1,000 pounds more on your back. Your brain is on its sixth cup of coffee, but you haven't had a drop of caffeine. Grief is like running a marathon while standing still. Like the ocean tide, coming and going.

That is how I felt in the fall of 2019. Lexie, my beloved dog of almost 17 years, passed away in my arms. It was late in the night, so I laid her covered up in her dog bed until I could take her to be cremated in the morning.

I sat alone on my bed, tears pouring out of my body as I had never experienced heartbreak this bad. During every surgery I recovered from, she sat next to me. When I had my hysterectomy, Lexie had walked down and around me on the bed to not walk over my stomach -- as if she knew.

I called her *"My ohana; My heartbeat."* She was my little lucky charm, as I got her on St. Patrick's Day. I was 19, and I truly did not know the impact she would have on my life. She was with me through all of the good days and bad days -- through building my business, illness, car rides, boating, kayaking and so much more. Now, she was gone.

That night as I was getting through my half-assed bedtime routine, I looked over at a gratitude journal I had written in every night for several years.

I didn't want to write in it. I was exhausted. I was broken.

I picked up the journal, trying to avoid staining the pages with tears, and wrote down the things I was thankful for that day on one of the worst days of my life. I choke back tears now, with a lump in my throat, remembering how fucking hard it was to do that.

I cried myself to sleep. That morning, I drove her to be cremated. I didn't want to go home, so I went and walked at the park I use to take her to. I had never been at home without her. For almost half my life, she was always at the door to greet me.

As I returned home from the park, I was greeted at my door with a phone call. As I turned the key in the lock, my father called to tell me that my aunt lost her battle with an ongoing illness. It hadn't even been 12 hours, and I had to deal with a second death.

My body became numb. The tears drained from my eyes without a single thought; I was broken-hearted. That night as I climbed into bed, there sat next to me my gratitude journal.

"How can I find something to be grateful for now?" After another day of heartbreak, I carefully let the ink glide

across the lines. Exhausted but unable to sleep, I grabbed my laptop.

It had been on my to-do list for years to design and create my own gratitude journal that I could put in my studio shop, but time always got away from me.

Dealing with the grief from the death of my dog and aunt, I had canceled all my clients' appointments that week. I now had the time to create the gratitude journal. I started working away at what I wanted it to look like -- the text, the lines, the style, the vibe, and the dedication page. I worked into the morning and throughout the day. I was going to do this, and I was going to do it now.

I figured if I could find gratitude in the storm, others could benefit from a journal, too. I worked on it for two days, barely sleeping. I sent it off to the printer and had it published just before my aunt's funeral on Halloween.

Gratitude is simple but so good for your soul. We say thank you when someone holds a door open for us, when we receive a gift, and when someone pays us a compliment. We are taught as a child to say *"thank you"* when someone does something for us. A gratitude journal helps expand that thinking into your everyday life.

I had gone full-time with my photography business, just after my sinus and nose reconstruction surgeries, when I first started writing in a gratitude journal. That's when I knew I wanted to create my own journal.

Every day, you simply write five things you are thankful for. You may think it is easy as you think to yourself *"family, food, shelter, job, friends."* But try that every day for a year. Try it on the worst days of your life. It changes you, for the better.

Expand on little details throughout the day. Examples like:

"I am grateful the lady at the store let me go ahead of her so I could get home sooner."

"I am grateful that my friend called to check on me."

"I am grateful it rained and watered my flowers."

"I am grateful for the compliment I received at the bank."

"I am grateful I was able to take a nap before dinner with my friends."

The first two weeks seemed easy, then each day was harder.

"What was I thankful for today?"

I really started struggling.

"Do I really not have anything to be thankful for today?"

I would recap the day in my head searching for little things to be thankful for that I may have forgotten.

Then I started noticing a shift within myself. As I woke up each day, I would make a point when something happened to think to myself, *"I need to make sure to write that in my journal tonight."*

That is when it started clicking. Everyone that spoke about gratitude journals always seemed to know something I didn't, as if they had some secret key to an unknown world of contentment.

Sure, I can say I am grateful for things, but I started FEELING grateful all day long. I was LOOKING for things to be thankful for each day instead of focusing on what I didn't have.

As I started researching things, I discovered that practicing gratitude rewires your brain to help you deal with and process the current situation and circumstances. It increases your mind's awareness and broader perception. It can help reduce symptoms of stress, depression, and anxiety at a neurological level. It increases the prefrontal cortex, which helps manage negative emotions.

I wish I would have known this sooner.

My mind, body, and business started shifting for the better. In the past, I had been so consumed with the pain; that slipped into survival mode, and I didn't even know it.

Gratitude was pulling me out of the darkness.

CHAPTER 14

Leveling Up

Taking long walks may be one of my favorite things to do to zone out. I listen to music, enjoy nature, or put on a great audiobook. Especially since, at one point in time, even walking to the restroom required a pep talk and a plan of action.

One day a few years ago, my thoughts became very clear mid-stride. I stopped dead in my tracks as a light bulb went off in my head.

If you got food poising from a restaurant, would you go back? Maybe once just to try it again? Maybe a few times?

Maybe not at all? Would you be hesitant to eat there again?

If you went back to try it again and kept getting food poisoning, would you keep going?

No!

So why do you keep going back to situations *(friends, family, jobs, doctors, etc.)* that are poisoning you?

You wouldn't watch the same movie every day if you

didn't like it. So why give the same energy to living the same life you don't like?

Writing a new script isn't something done instantly but is done with each choice we make.

Different experiences require different reactions. A time to heal, a time to grieve, a time to be sick, and a time to be healthy. A time to hurt, to love, and to learn.

At one point, I got the tattoo "everything happens for a reason" on my right forearm in reference to Ecclesiastic 3.

> There is a time for everything,
>> and a season for every activity under the heavens
> ² a time to be born and a time to die,
>> a time to plant and a time to uproot,
> ³ a time to kill and a time to heal,
>> a time to tear down and a time to build,
> ⁴ a time to weep and a time to laugh,
>> a time to mourn and a time to dance,
> ⁵ a time to scatter stones and a time to gather them,
>> a time to embrace and a time to refrain from embracing,
> ⁶ a time to search and a time to give up,
>> a time to keep and a time to throw away,
> ⁷ a time to tear and a time to mend,
>> a time to be silent and a time to speak,
> ⁸ a time to love and a time to hate,
>> a time for war and a time for peace.

It may not make sense to us at the time, but I believe there is a reason why it happened. I have learned from or am continuing to learn from each one of my life experiences. It may take years to fully learn from, but I level up with each lesson.

I talk a lot about "leveling up." The higher up the mountain you go, the thicker the air is and the harder it gets to breathe -- but it results in the best view.

Sometimes when I tell people about the situations I have been through, they seem shocked. Other times I hear, *"Oh my gosh that happened to me too!"*

Our life experiences play a role in our perception. A 10-pound weight is still a 10-pound weight to a bodybuilder as it is to a small child. What we carry is part of what makes us who we are, and why everything happens for a reason. While the weight may be easy for you, it might be harder for someone else.

Get comfortable with getting uncomfortable. Get so sick of your own shit that you decide: *"This isn't the life I want."*

Or, get sick of everyone else's shit. Quit the job, open the business, call off the wedding, send the text, book the flight, sign on the dotted line, buy the boat, lose the weight, gain the weight, apply for the job, whatever it is that is holding you back...

Whatever excuse that came to your head -- that thing you have been putting off -- that is what is keeping you from leveling up and preventing you from taking action. I picture it in my mind like a ladder, just start climbing and don't look down.

Each step you take in life takes you higher, and you start leveling up.

CHAPTER 15

You Can't Save the World at Midnight

If you are anything like me when you're sleepy, you get ready for bed. As soon as your head hits the pillow, your brain is wide awake. You count the hours, *"If I fall asleep now, I will get five hours of sleep."*

Just as you think you are about to go into a deep slumber, you get another idea or thought.

I always have to remind myself; *"You can't save the world at midnight."*

Just like Rome wasn't built in a day.

While I shared parts of my story with you. From my jumping on a bed at 3 years old to bullying to endometriosis. I told you about losing 100 pounds, sinus and nose reconstruction, going full time as a small business owner, going sepsis, and opening my photography studio.

I learned to cut toxic people and things out of my life, to find my fears and lean into them, to draw closer to God, and to practice gratitude.

None of that happened overnight.

Not a single one of those things! …and it certainly didn't happen at midnight. It took weeks, months, and even years.

We are a work in progress.

Some days I still feel the heartbreak of not being able to carry a child on my own. I look in the mirror and see the body of a woman in her 30s that menopause has aged before its time. I watch videos on TikTok of birth announcements and adoption stories. I see videos of women trying to get answers from doctors that are dismissing endometriosis. At times, I fight with myself to talk about it, because it changed me so much, and sometimes want to forget the emptiness it left in my life. The pictures painted in my head of the life I wanted were smeared with the reality of the life I have and have to make the best of it.

The old question of "Where do you see yourself in five years?" plagued my generation (and the ones before mine).

I remember at 18 daydreaming of having a big house, watching the kids' football practice, and having a loving husband to come home to. Vacations and trips to the beach. I needed to marry before 23 and have children at 25. I wanted to be a part-time photographer and write books while raising twin boys that I had already picked out names for. Maybe we had a dog or two.

I had no idea when I was 3 years old that jumping on a bed would affect the whole course of my life. I had no idea when I was age 12 laying on the bathroom floor hunched over in agony that the pain would last 13 years and end with a seven-inch scar and leave me childless. I had no idea that I would wake up one day and have a whole new look to my face.

I had to let go of the life I had in order to build a new dream. For a while, I was in a cycle of sadness and carried around trauma in my coat pocket pretending it wasn't there. I moved on, but not forward. Now I acknowledge my feelings and address my emotions.

I feel so grateful now to look back and see the things I once prayed for and asked God and the universe for, that have now come to fruition. I have learned that where the focus goes is where the energy flows.

At times throughout my journey, I was letting the events control my life – instead of me controlling the events in my life.

For a while, I had forgotten to plan for the future and was living day-to-day.

Now, I have learned to look forward to the future.

CHAPTER 16

The Next Chapter

So here we are. Please wait until the ride comes to a complete stop before taking off your safety belt and exiting the ride.

My life has felt like a roller coaster, with highs and lows. Sometimes I look back on my life, and the memories feel so distant. I don't really remember that girl. Other times, I remember the experiences vividly -- almost as if they happened yesterday.

Shifting my perspective is what taught me to see things differently. Life is so unpredictable. We never know what tomorrow will bring. What life-altering surgery you will have, what decision you will have to make, what dream you will have to let go of, and what new dreams you get to create. Even what you look like tomorrow can completely change overnight.

Before I started selling off my furniture to build my business, I was sitting on my couch watching my dog, Lexie, she walked down the hallway and lay on the floor. Mind you, my apartment is only 22 steps long -- so not much of a hallway. It was an odd place for her to plop down, especially when she was right next to me all the time. She did this for several days and each time I watched her, puzzled.

Curiosity got the best of me one afternoon. I went and sat down next to her, asking, "Why are you sitting here all by yourself? Of all the places, in the middle of the hallway?"

I sat there petting her for a solid 10 minutes; she laid her head down and went to sleep. As she drifted off to sleep, I sat there quietly and in a moment of peace myself.

The heat kicked on. A blast of hot air fell from the vents above us. I smiled and chuckled. She knew where the heat was and got cozy warm when she wanted to take a nap.

I had to change my perspective and be patient to get my answers. If I would have never changed my view and sat next to her, I wouldn't have known.

One of the things I teach when I mentor other photographers who get a new camera is to find a tree. I tell them to photograph it every day, whether it is raining, snowing, leaves falling, or leaves blooming. The tree stays in the same exact spot but the lighting and weather changes. The roots become deeper; the tree becomes taller. Each day it is the same tree, the situations are different. Not only does the tree grow each day, but the photographer does. The photographer learns what time, lighting, lens, and what setting is best. The perspective changes, and the perspective of the photographer changes too.

Remember when I talked about focusing on everything that was red in the room, then asked what you saw that was yellow? Life is ever-changing. Your health may never get better or you may be cured tomorrow. Your business may fail or may blow up to seven figures tomorrow. We just don't know. By focusing on gratitude and taking action, we can shift our focus and change our perspectives. All those terrible things that happen to us can teach us, shape us, and help us grow. Not only us but the people around us.

I started writing this book when I was in the thick of the shit with endometriosis. I kept putting it off.

"Oh, I need to be here in life before I can finish it. I want to have made this much money before I write it. I want to be a mom before I do it. I want to be out of my apartment that I talk about in the first chapter before I publish it."

(Spoiler alert, I am still in that same apartment. Still no couch! My living room is a gorgeous office space now.)

If I kept waiting for the right time, it would never be the right time.

We can have an idea in our head of who we want to be, when we want to do something, and at what age we want it by. Sometimes those things materialize, and sometimes something completely different transpires.

That teacher that said I would never be an artist? I've been a photographer for 22 years and won dozens of awards -- some even internationally. The people that said I couldn't own my business, they were wrong too. So many people will tell you that you aren't capable of something -- because *they* aren't. You are capable of so many things.

You may be sitting on a book idea or a job you want. You may be laying in bed with endometriosis and a heating pad. Maybe you were bullied or have a business idea someone told you couldn't do.

Whatever it is, I believe in you. Don't give up! You don't know how close you are.

While we all have chapters that we don't read out loud, I am grateful that you read some of mine. I hope the stories made you feel less alone, inspired you, or provoked a dream in you.

Life will take us on a journey of unpredictable things. Although I am not right where I felt I needed to be when finishing this book, thankfully, I have learned I am right where I am supposed to be.

Now, I am looking forward to the seventeenth chapter.

Message to Endometriosis Warriors

Dear Endo Sisters,

I see the pain you hide behind the makeup. The dozens of tampons and pads you have to buy every month. The heating pads are always close by. The fact that you know how many miles it is to the closest hospital and that you know what veins are best for your IV. The friendships you have lost, the relationships that have ended. The miscarriages you have had, infertility you struggle with. I see you.

The sharp pains that have brought you to your knees. The hemorrhaging that you have experienced. The days you have lost from laying in bed or in a fog of pain medications. The barbed wire pains that have paralyzed your body, but make you feel every ounce of sheer pain. The surgeries you had to have, the medical bills, the insurance calls, the debt collector calls. The pills, the problems that turn into addictions, suicides, and the loneliness of battling an illness that people that don't know – just don't understand. I see you.

I pray that there will be a cure one day that will give you back your life. That new treatments come out and can help you. That the right doctors are placed in your path to help you.

That your relationships flourish, your friendships stay strong, and that your dreams are always a front runner.

And if the day comes and your dreams have to change, or you have to sign on the dotted line for a hysterectomy. Or you hear a baby cry and it's not yours, just know I am there with you and you are so strong and brave. I see you.

- Joslyn

AFFIRMATION FROM THE AUTHOR

"When I was a little girl, I dreamed of many things. As I become older, they slowly slipped away. Life moved fast and yet so slow. The days passed by and so did my life. I lost who I was over and over again. When I finally found myself, I vowed to stay true to myself.

To love me. To love others. To not be conformed to the lines that others drew around me. To be strong in adversity. To always get back up and hold my head up strong.

To fail, and to fail often, and to take those lessons and grow to the best version of myself. To let go of the dreams I had as a little girl and make dreams as the woman I have become. To take adventures and discover new things I love. To do something every day different and do things that make my life better.

Today I dream of living a healthy life full of abundance and love. To be surrounded by light and love and to be the light. To be closer to God and live a fulfilled life. To trust His plan, even if it isn't my own. To love like I've never been hurt and do fun things, even if I do them alone. To be the best version of myself. To be a dreamer in a sleepless world."

Joslyn D. Crowl

www.ingramcontent.com/pod-product-compliance
Lightning Source LLC
Chambersburg PA
CBHW052322220526
45472CB00001B/235